Cockroaches

by L. Patricia Kite

Lerner Publications Company • Minneapolis, Minnesota

To Robert San Souci, a forever friend, whose
unending kindness is very much appreciated

Thanks to our series consultant, Sharyn Fenwick, elementary science and math specialist. Mrs.
Fenwick was the winner of the National Science Teachers Association 1991 Distinguished
Teaching Award. She also was the recipient of the Presidential Award for Excellence in Math
and Science Teaching, representing the state of Minnesota at the elementary level in 1992.

Photographs are reproduced with the permission of the following sources: © Robert and Linda
Mitchell, front cover, pp. 4, 5, 6, 8, 9, 10, 11, 12, 13, 14, 15, 16 (both), 17, 19 (both),
20, 22, 25, 26, 27, 28, 29, 30, 31, 32, 33, 35, 38, 41, 43, 46–47; © Dwight R. Kuhn, p. 7;
© G/C Merker/Visuals Unlimited, p. 21; © David T. Roberts/Nature's Images/Photo Researchers
Inc., p. 23; © SIU/Visuals Unlimited, p. 24, © W. J. Weber/Visuals Unlimited, p. 34;
© D. Cavagnaro/Visuals Unlimited, p. 35; © J. H. Robinson/Photo Researchers Inc., p. 37;
Minneapolis Public Library and Information Center, p. 39; © Kim Fennema/Visuals Unlimited,
p. 40; AP/Wide World Photos, p. 42.

Text copyright © 2001 by L. Patricia Kite

Early Bird Nature Books were conceptualized by Ruth Berman
and designed by Steve Foley. Series editor is Joelle Riley.

Website address: www.lernerbooks.com

Lerner Publications Company
A division of Lerner Publishing Group
241 First Avenue North
Minneapolis, Minnesota 55401 U.S.A.

Library of Congress Cataloging-in-Publication Data

Kite, L. Patricia.
    Cockroaches / by L. Patricia Kite.
        p.   cm. — (Early bird nature books)
    Summary: Describes the cockroach's life cycle, behavior,
habitat, and interaction with humans.
    ISBN 0-8225-3046-5 (lib. bdg. : alk. paper)
    1. Cockroaches—Juvenile literature. [1. Cockroaches.]
I. Title. II. Series.
QL505.5.K586 2001
595.7'28—dc21   00-8906

Manufactured in the United States of America
1 2 3 4 5 6 – JR – 06 05 04 03 02 01

Contents

Be a Word Detective

Can you find these words as you read about the cockroach's life? Be a detective and try to figure out what they mean. You can turn to the glossary on page 46 for help.

abdomen	**exoskeleton**	**ootheca**
antennas	**mandibles**	**palpi**
cerci	**molting**	**spiracles**
compound eyes	**nymph**	**thorax**

There is more than one way to form plurals of some words. The word antenna has two possible plural endings—either an e or an s. In this book, s is used when many antennas are being discussed.

5

There are over 3,500 species, or kinds, of cockroaches. This is a brown-banded cockroach. Do most cockroaches live near people?

Cockroaches Everywhere

 Many people don't like cockroaches. People don't want cockroaches near them. But most cockroaches do not live near people. They live in the wild.

Cockroaches are amazing creatures. Some can go without food for three weeks. Some can survive freezing cold. Others can live in blazing heat.

Cockroaches are insects. All insects have six legs. And they have three main body parts. They have a head, a thorax, and an abdomen (AB-duh-muhn).

Grasshoppers are relatives of cockroaches.

Cockroaches live all over the world. Most species live in warm and damp places, such as tropical forests. Other species of cockroaches live in mountains, deserts, grasslands, and swamps. Some species of cockroaches live where people live. We call these species pests.

Death's head cockroaches live in Central America.
Cockroaches are also called roaches.

This colorful cockroach lives in a tropical forest.

Most cockroaches are brown or black. But some species are brightly colored. They are green, orange, or other colors. Some roaches have bright stripes. Others have spots.

One of the biggest cockroaches in the world is called the giant cockroach.

Different species of cockroaches are different sizes. The smallest roaches are the size of a tomato seed. The biggest roaches are the size of a small mouse.

Cockroaches are usually safe in dark places.

Almost all roaches avoid light. They spend
the day resting and hiding. During the day,
they hide even if they are hungry. But when it
gets dark, cockroaches come out to look for food.

Chapter 2

This German cockroach's scientific name is Blatella germanica. *What shape is a roach's body?*

Body Parts

 Cockroaches have flat, oval bodies.
This shape helps roaches hide in small holes.
They can also slide through narrow cracks.

On its head, a roach has two long, thin antennas (an-TEH-nuhz). Roaches use their antennas for smell and touch. The antennas have thousands of little hairs on them. The hairs help the roaches to smell and feel objects.

A cockroach's mouth has mandibles (MAN-duh-buhlz). Mandibles are sharp jaws. They have tiny, strong teeth. The teeth can scrape and chew food.

A cockroach uses its antennas to feel the temperature around it.

Next to the cockroach's mouth are four feelers. The feelers are called palpi (PAL-peye). Palpi are covered with tiny bristles. A cockroach uses the bristles on the palpi to taste food.

A cockroach's four palpi are next to its mouth.

This cockroach's simple eyes are next to its antennas.
Simple eyes can sense light and dark.

Cockroaches have two large eyes. They are just behind the antennas. The eyes are called compound eyes. Compound eyes are made up of many small eyes.

Some species of cockroaches have two extra eyes. These eyes are smaller than the compound eyes. The small eyes are called simple eyes.

A cockroach's legs have many special parts. These parts can sense objects moving near the roach.
Inset: Stiff leg hairs help to sense motion.

Behind a roach's head is its thorax. Six legs are attached to the thorax. The legs are covered with stiff hairs. At the end of each leg are two claws. A cockroach uses its claws to hold on to ceilings and walls.

Many species of cockroaches have two pairs of wings on their thorax. Some of these roaches can fly. But other roaches who have wings cannot fly.

If a cockroach has wings, the front pair are stiffer than the back pair.

antenna

simple eye

compound eye

mandible

palpi

head

legs

thorax

abdomen

wings

cerci

The Parts of a Cockroach's Body

A cockroach uses its cerci to sense objects moving nearby.
Inset: *This is a close-up of a roach's cerci.*

The largest part of a cockroach's body is its abdomen. The abdomen is behind the thorax. At the end of a cockroach's abdomen are two cerci (SUHR-seye). Cerci are stubby feelers. Cerci have tiny hairs all over them. These hairs sense even the smallest air movements. Moving air warns the cockroach that danger might be near. When a roach feels air move, it darts away.

Cockroaches have an exoskeleton (ek-soh-SKEH-luh-tuhn). The exoskeleton is a hard shell that covers a roach's whole body. The exoskeleton protects the cockroach from harm.

A roach's exoskeleton is waxy. This helps to keep the roach from soaking up water.

Spiracles are the holes running along a roach's body.

Cockroaches breathe through spiracles (SPIHR-ih-kuhlz). The spiracles are 20 holes in the roach's exoskeleton. Four of the spiracles are on top of the cockroach's thorax. The rest of the spiracles are on the sides of the abdomen.

Chapter 3

Oriental cockroaches are busy eating a rotten potato. Do roaches need to drink water?

They'll Eat Anything!

 Cockroaches eat just about anything. They eat rotten wood, dead animals, other insects, paper, and glue. They eat computer wires, animal droppings, soap, vegetables, grease, candy, paint, and dog food.

Cockroaches need to drink plenty of water. Without water, they dry up and die. A few species of roaches can live two or three weeks without any water. These roaches can live even longer without food.

An American cockroach feasts on a sandwich.

Before a cockroach eats, it tastes its food. But it doesn't taste the food with its mouth. It tastes the food with its palpi. Tasting food first is important because people sometimes try to poison roaches. Roaches can taste poison with their palpi before they swallow it. This way, cockroaches can avoid eating poison.

People can buy all sorts of poisons to try to kill cockroaches.

This American cockroach is cleaning its leg.

Cockroaches clean themselves often. They make sure their hairs and feelers are clean. If these body parts are not clean, the roach can't smell, taste, or feel objects well.

Chapter 4

Some female cockroaches lay thousands of eggs in their lifetime. What does a roach put her eggs in?

From Eggs to Adults

Most species of cockroaches lay eggs. Some species lay eggs only once or twice in their lifetime. But some species of roaches lay eggs many times.

A female Oriental cockroach's ootheca. The ootheca protects the eggs inside.

A female cockroach lays her eggs in an ootheca (oh-uh-THEE-kuh). An ootheca is a strong sac. The cockroach makes the ootheca from chemicals inside her body.

Each species of cockroach lays a different number of eggs at a time. Some oothecas contain only 16 eggs. Some contain as many as 44 eggs.

A roach's ootheca often sticks out from the end of her abdomen.

Some species of cockroaches leave the ootheca in a safe place. Then the adults leave. Other species carry the ootheca under their body for a while.

The baby cockroaches grow within the ootheca. When they are ready to hatch, the babies swallow lots of air. The air makes the babies fat. They get so fat that the ootheca splits. Then the babies can get out.

A female Madagascan hissing cockroach protects her babies after they have hatched. This species of roach can make hissing noises.

A young cockroach is called a nymph (NIHMF). Nymphs look a lot like adult cockroaches. But a nymph's antennas and cerci are much shorter than an adult's. And nymphs have no wings. At first, a nymph's exoskeleton is clear. But soon the nymph's color changes to the same color as its parents.

These are American cockroach nymphs. This species of roach lives for about one year.

This cockroach is molting.

As a nymph grows, its exoskeleton becomes too tight. The nymph must shed its old exoskeleton. Shedding an old skin is called molting. To begin molting, a cockroach gulps air. Its exoskeleton becomes tighter and tighter. Then it splits down the middle. Underneath is a new, soft exoskeleton. In just a few hours, the new exoskeleton becomes hard.

This Madagascan hissing cockroach is white because it has just molted.

Different species of roaches molt different numbers of times. Some species molt only 6 times in their lifetime. Other species may molt as many as 12 times.

After its last molt, a cockroach looks just like its parents. It is an adult.

Different species of nymphs need different amounts of time to grow up. Some become adults in about 50 days. Others take more than one year to become adults. Roaches live from six months to five years after their last molt.

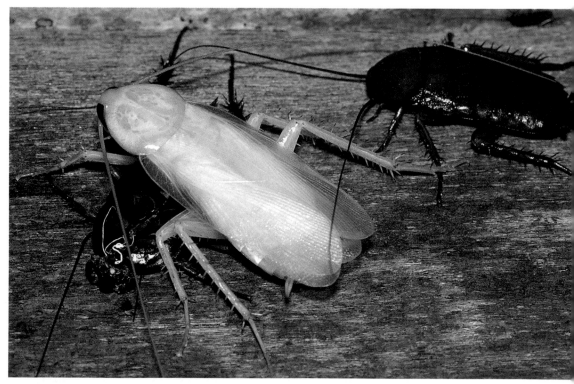

This roach has just finished its final molt. You can tell that it is an adult because it has wings.

Chapter 5

One enemy of cockroaches is a lizard called an anole. Anoles eat cockroaches. What other animals eat cockroaches?

Dangers to Cockroaches

 Many animals eat cockroaches. Birds, snakes, mice, wasps, and toads all eat them. Centipedes, scorpions, tarantulas, and lizards eat roaches, too.

Even if a cockroach has wings, it does not use them to escape from enemies. The roach uses its legs to run away.

Cockroaches have many ways to protect themselves. Roaches are hard to see because they usually move around in the dark. They can tell when something moves nearby. If an enemy is near, roaches can hide in a tiny place. And roaches can run away very quickly. A cockroach can start running before a person can blink.

Cockroaches leave a bad smell wherever they go. Some animals may avoid roaches because of this.

A few species of roaches have special ways to protect themselves. Some give off a stinky odor when something bothers them. One species rolls up into a ball when it is attacked.

Scorpions are enemies of cockroaches.

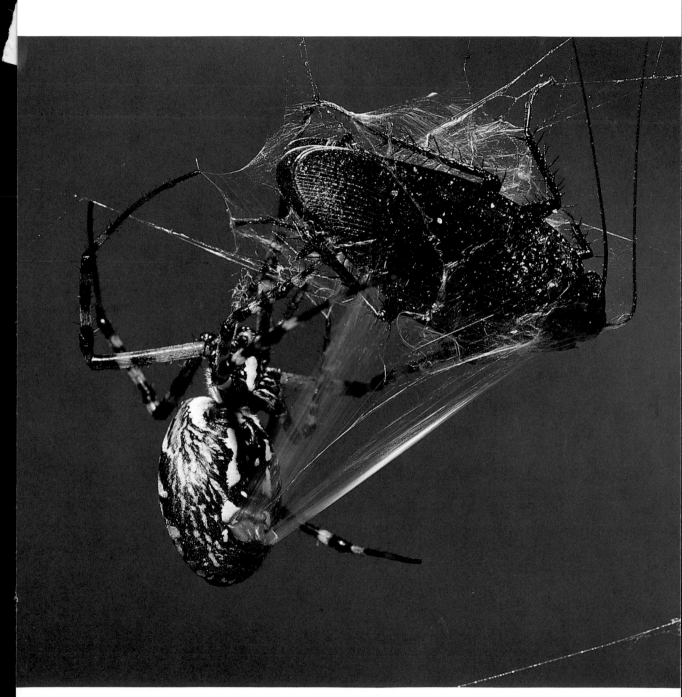

This roach is stuck in a spider's sticky web.

Chapter 6

Cockroaches look much the same as they did long, long ago. Have roaches always lived all over the world?

Cockroaches and People

Cockroaches have been around longer than most other kinds of insects. They lived on the earth even before the dinosaurs did. Cockroaches look much the same now as they did long ago.

Ships carry roaches all over the world.

Cockroaches first lived in warm, damp areas. But many years ago, some species of roaches began to travel with people. They crawled aboard ships. They went ashore when the ships landed. The roaches began to live in new places.

Roaches still hide aboard ships. They hide on airplanes, too. This way, roaches travel all over the world.

Sometimes people don't even notice a roach crawling on their food.

Cockroaches who live in people's homes, restaurants, or stores are pests. Cockroaches walk in garbage and dirty places. Some of the dirt sticks to the roaches. Later, the roaches may

Cockroaches may spread germs by leaving their droppings on people's food.

walk on human food or belongings. They get dirt on people's things. Most people believe roaches spread diseases this way. But some scientists do not agree with this idea.

Some people keep cockroaches as pets. This pet roach lives in the country of Australia.

Cockroaches who live in the tropics help some plants to stay alive.

Most cockroaches live in nature. They do not bother people. Many of these roaches eat dead plants and animals. They help to clean the earth. In this way, cockroaches are an important part of nature.

On Sharing a Book

As you know, adults greatly influence a child's attitude toward reading. When a child sees you read, or when you share a book with a child, you're sending a message that reading is important. Show the child that reading a book together is important to you. Find a comfortable, quiet place. Turn off the television and limit other distractions, such as telephone calls.

Be prepared to start slowly. Take turns reading parts of this book. Stop and talk about what you're reading. Talk about the photographs. You may find that much of the shared time is spent discussing just a few pages. This discussion time is valuable for both of you, so don't move through the book too quickly. If the child begins to lose interest, stop reading. Continue sharing the book at another time. When you do pick up the book again, be sure to revisit the parts you have already read. Most importantly, enjoy the book!

Be a Vocabulary Detective

You will find a word list on page 5. Words selected for this list are important to the understanding of the topic of this book. Encourage the child to be a word detective and search for the words as you read the book together. Talk about what the words mean and how they are used in the sentence. Do any of these words have more than one meaning? You will find these words defined in a glossary on page 46.

What about Questions?

Use questions to make sure the child understands the information in this book. Here are some suggestions:

> What did this paragraph tell us? What does this picture show? What do you think we'll learn about next? What kind of animal is a cockroach? Do most roaches live in the same places as people do? What shape is a cockroach's body? How many wings do cockroaches have? What do roaches eat? How can a roach taste food without eating it? What is a baby cockroach called? What animal enemies do roaches have? How do cockroaches protect themselves from enemies? How have roaches traveled around the world? What is your favorite part of the book? Why?

If the child has questions, don't hesitate to respond with questions of your own, such as: What do *you* think? Why? What is it that you don't know? If the child can't remember certain facts, turn to the index.

Introducing the Index

The index is an important learning tool. It helps readers get information quickly without searching throughout the whole book. Turn to the index on page 47. Choose an entry, such as *eating*, and ask the child to use the index to find out what a cockroach eats. Repeat this exercise with as many entries as you like. Ask the child to point out the differences between an index and a glossary. (The index helps readers find information quickly, while the glossary tells readers what words mean.)

All the World in Metric!

Although our monetary system is in metric units (based on multiples of 10), the United States is one of the few countries in the world that does not use the metric system of measurement. Here are some conversion activities you and the child can do using a calculator:

WHEN YOU KNOW:	MULTIPLY BY:	TO FIND:
miles	1.609	kilometers
feet	0.3048	meters
inches	2.54	centimeters
gallons	3.787	liters
tons	0.907	metric tons
pounds	0.454	kilograms

Activities

Make up a story about a cockroach. Be sure to include information from this book. Draw or paint pictures to illustrate your story.

Cockroaches are called different things in different countries. For example, in Japan they are called "abula mushi." Go to the library and find out what they are called in five other countries. Find out exactly what these names mean.

Sometimes people keep cockroaches as pets. One famous pet cockroach species is the Madagascan hissing cockroach. Find out if anybody you know has a pet roach. Ask if you can visit the roach. Or go to a pet store and see if they sell cockroaches. See if you can identify the different body parts described in this book.

Glossary

abdomen (AB-duh-muhn)—the back part of a cockroach's body

antennas (an-TEH-nuhz)—the feelers on a cockroach's head

cerci (SUHR-seye)—the stubby feelers at the end of a cockroach's body

compound eyes—eyes made up of many small eyes

exoskeleton (ek-soh-SKEH-luh-tuhn)—a hard shell that covers a cockroach's body

mandibles (MAN-duh-buhlz)—a cockroach's sharp jaws.

molting—shedding old skin to make way for a new, larger skin

nymph (NIHMF)—a baby cockroach

ootheca (oh-uh-THEE-kuh)—a strong sac in which a female cockroach lays her eggs

palpi (PAL-peye)—the four feelers next to a cockroach's mouth

spiracles (SPIHR-ih-kuhlz)—breathing holes on the side of a cockroach's body

thorax—the middle part of a cockroach's body

Index

Pages listed in **bold** type
refer to photographs.

About the Author

L. Patricia "Pat" Kite became fascinated with insects upon discovering that female earwigs were very careful mothers. The more Pat learned about insects, the more interested she became. She has a special love for research—especially in the fields of biology and biography. Pat holds a teaching credential in biology and social science, and a master's degree in journalism. She is a New York native but has spent the last 30 years in Newark, California, where she raised four children as a single parent. Pat's hobbies include gardening, reading, meandering, distance walking, local politics, and volunteering at the local wildlife rehabilitation center.

The Early Bird Nature Books Series

African Elephants	Horses	Sandhill Cranes
Alligators	Jellyfish	Scorpions
Ants	Manatees	Sea Lions
Apple Trees	Moose	Sea Turtles
Bobcats	Mountain Goats	Slugs
Brown Bears	Mountain Gorillas	Swans
Cats	Peacocks	Tarantulas
Cockroaches	Penguins	Tigers
Cougars	Polar Bears	Venus Flytraps
Crayfish	Popcorn Plants	Vultures
Dandelions	Prairie Dogs	Walruses
Dolphins	Rats	Whales
Giant Sequoia Trees	Red-Eyed Tree Frogs	White-Tailed Deer
Herons	Saguaro Cactus	Wild Turkeys